I0558225

our

last

goodbye

the end of us – echoes of lost love

Tender Tulip

Tender Tulip

Paperback ISBN: 978-1-961902-06-0

Printed in the United States of America

Cover design by Temika Mccanns

Editor and Illustrator: Elsie Bloomfield

It ends with us

Contents

Tender Tulip

He promised me forever

But forever was just a lie

I gave him my love

But all he gave me was goodbye

I thought I was special

But I was just another chapter

In his book of manipulation

And emotional disaster

I was blinded by his words

But now I see the truth

I was just a pawn

In his game of youth

I thought love was enough

But now I know better

Love should never hurt

It should bring you to your feet, not tether

It ends with us

But what is love

When it's not love at all

But a cycle of abuse

That leaves you bruised and small?

The end was just the start

Of my journey to healing

But the question remains

Is love worth the feeling?

melancholy

It ends with us

i am the girl

who wears her heart

on her sleeve

for all to see

Tender Tulip

i am the girl

who wears my pain

like a badge of honor

It ends with us

i am the girl

who has known

the depths of melancholy

but i am also

the girl

who has risen

from the ashes

i've been to the bottom

of the ocean

where the darkness is thick

and the pressure is heavy

Tender Tulip

i've been to the edge

of the cliff

where the wind howls

and the fear is real

It ends with us

i've been to the depths

of melancholy

and i've come back

with stories to tell

i've been to the place

where the shadows are long

and the light is dim

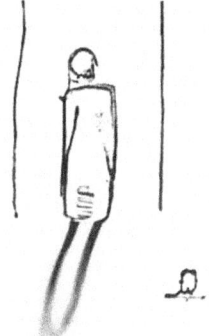

Tender Tulip

i've been to the place

where the tears are constant

and the pain is real

but i've also been to the place

where the strength is found

and the beauty is seen

even in the depths of melancholy

i know i will rise again

It ends with us

the weight of it all

presses down on my chest

a heavy feeling

of longing and loss

Tender Tulip

memories linger

like ghosts in my mind

reminding me

of what once was

i try to shake it off

but it clings to me

like a second skin

It ends with us

i try to find the light

but it eludes me

i am lost

in this sea of melancholy

but even in the darkness

i know i will find my way

to the other side

where the sun still shines

Tender Tulip

It ends with us

the leaves fall

from the trees

just like my heart

from my chest

i try to hold on

but it slips through my fingers

like sand

Tender Tulip

i try to numb the pain

but it still aches

like a wound that won't heal

It ends with us

memories linger

like a storm cloud

haunting me

i try to find peace

but it eludes me

Tender Tulip

i am lost

in this sea of melancholy

but even in the darkness

i know there is hope

It ends with us

a glimmer of light

that will guide me

to a brighter tomorrow

the sky is grey

like my soul

a reflection

of the pain inside

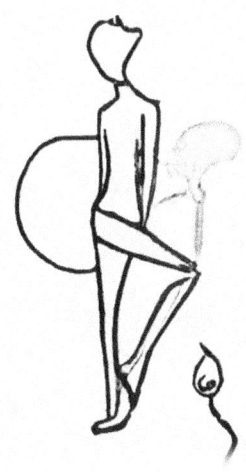

Tender Tulip

memories linger

like a bad dream

haunting me

It ends with us

i try to escape

but it follows me

like a shadow

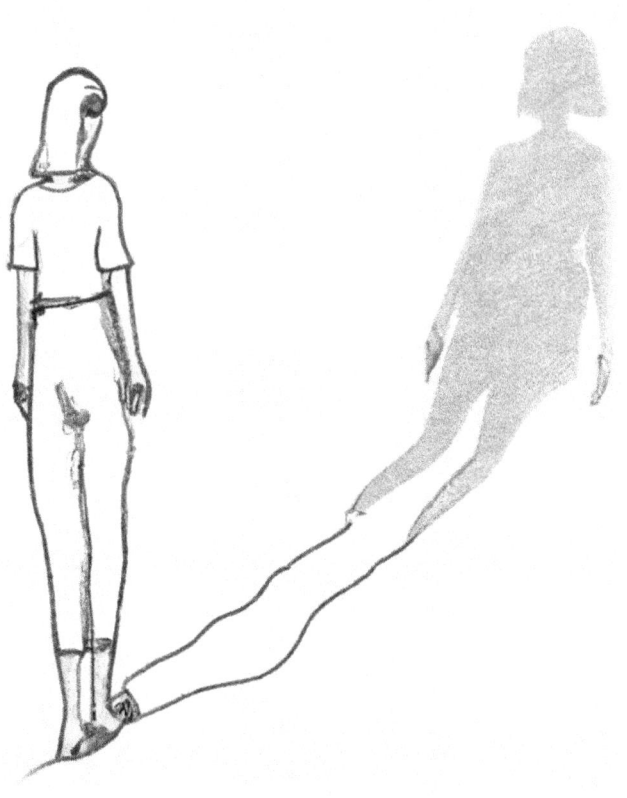

Tender Tulip

i try to find happiness

but it eludes me

i am lost

in this sea of melancholy

but even in the darkness

i know there is a way out

It ends with us

the tears fall

like rain

from my eyes

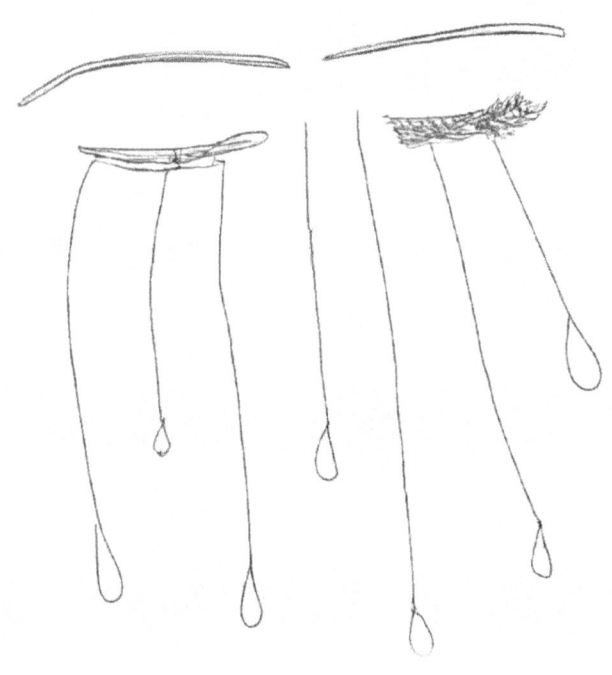

Tender Tulip

a constant reminder

of the pain

that won't go away

It ends with us

memories linger

like a bitter taste

on my tongue

Tender Tulip

i try to forget

but it clings to me

like a second skin

i am drowning

in this sea of melancholy

but even in the depths

i know there is a way out

It ends with us

the darkness closes in

like a cloak

around my shoulders

Tender Tulip

a constant companion

on this journey

of pain and loss

It ends with us

memories linger

like a whisper

in my ear

Tender Tulip

i try to silence them

but they echo

in my mind

i am lost

in this sea of melancholy

but even in the darkness

i know there is a way out

It ends with us

the nights are long

and the days are short

a reflection

of the emptiness inside

Tender Tulip

i try to fill the void

but it remains

like a gaping hole

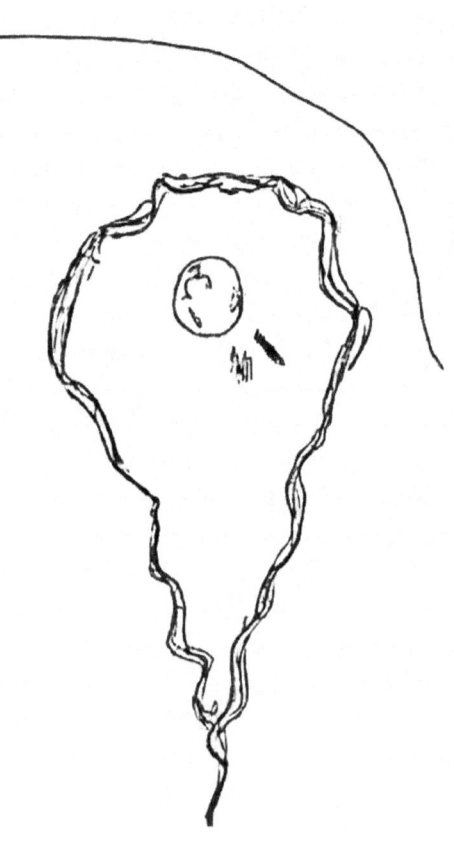

It ends with us

i try to move on

but the past clings

like a weight on my shoulders

i am lost

in this sea of melancholy

but even in the darkness

i know there is a way out

Tender Tulip

the sky is dark

the stars are hidden

a reflection

of the storm inside

It ends with us

i try to find the light

but it eludes me

like a mirage

Tender Tulip

i try to silence the noise

but the thoughts echo

like a broken record

i am trapped

in this sea of melancholy

but even in the depths

i know there is a way out

It ends with us

the world is spinning

but i am standing still

a reflection

of the numbness inside

Tender Tulip

i try to feel alive

but the emotions are distant

like a forgotten dream

It ends with us

i try to make sense

but the answers are elusive

like a puzzle with missing pieces

i am stuck

in this sea of melancholy

but even in the stagnation

i know there is a way out

hesitation

It ends with us

i sit in silence

hearing the whispers

of a past that once was

and a future that may be

Tender Tulip

i am torn between

fearing the unknown

and longing for the chance

to see what's yet to come

It ends with us

i know not what the future holds

but i fear the unknown

i am comfortable with the familiar

but change is necessary, it's shown

Tender Tulip

i am hesitant to take a step

afraid of falling and failing

i am stuck in this cycle

of self-doubt and wailing

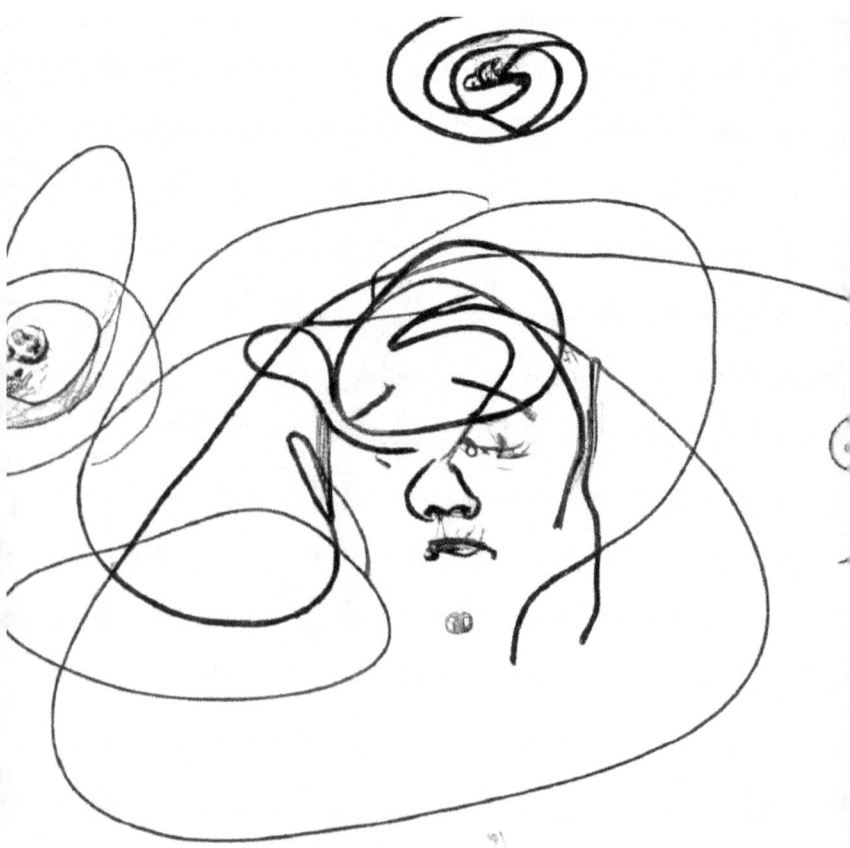

It ends with us

i am hesitant to trust

afraid of being hurt

i am hesitant to love

afraid of the pain it may bring

Tender Tulip

i am hesitant to let go

of the old, the comfortable

i am hesitant to embrace

the new, the unknown

It ends with us

i am hesitant to speak

afraid of being misunderstood

i am hesitant to follow

my heart, it's a path that's good

but hesitation is holding me back

from living and growing

i must take a leap of faith

and trust in my own knowing

Tender Tulip

i must let go of the past

and embrace the future

i must let go of fear

and hope, i must nurture

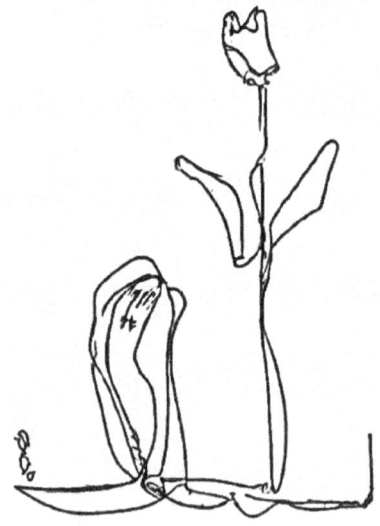

It ends with us

i must let go of control

and trust the journey

i must let go of the old

and welcome the new

Tender Tulip

i must let go of doubt

and trust in myself

i must let go of hesitation

and live in the present

It ends with us

i must speak my truth

and not fear judgment

i must follow my heart

and not fear the unknown

Tender Tulip

i must trust the journey

and not be afraid to take risks

i must let go of the past

and not let it hold me back

It ends with us

i must embrace change

and not be afraid to grow

i must trust in myself

and let my spirit flow

Tender Tulip

i've been stuck in this place

where the past and the future

collide

i've been stuck in this place

where the fear and the hope

coexist

It ends with us

i've been stuck in this place

where the what-ifs and the should-haves

cloud my mind

i've been stuck in this place

where the heart and the head

are at war

Tender Tulip

i've been stuck in this place

where the doubt and the trust

are in a constant battle

It ends with us

i've been stuck in this place

where the love and the hate

are intertwined

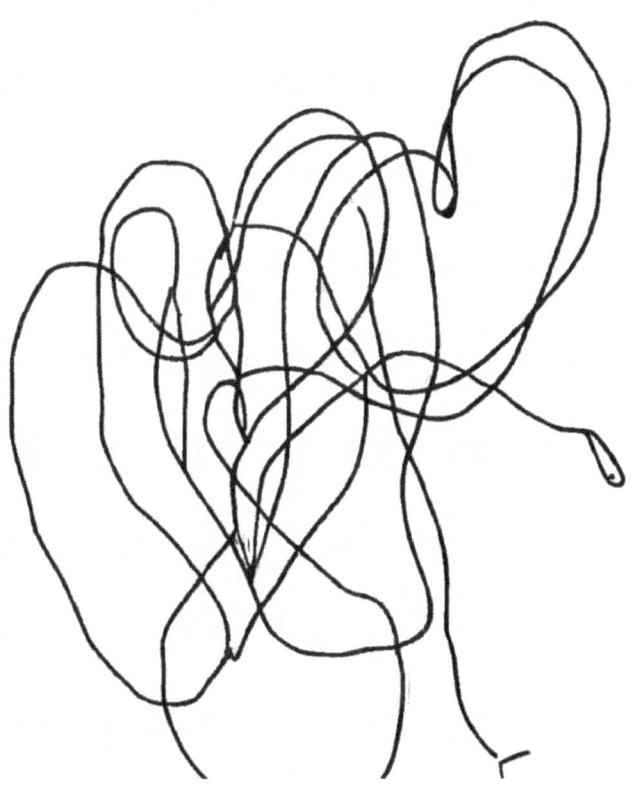

Tender Tulip

i am stuck in this moment

paralyzed by hesitation

i question every choice

and the path that i must take

It ends with us

i've been stuck in this place

where the old and the new

are constantly vying for attention

Tender Tulip

i've been stuck in this place

where the past and the future

are in a constant battle

It ends with us

i've been stuck in this place

where the present is

a fleeting moment

Tender Tulip

i've been stuck in this place

where the hesitation

is suffocating me

It ends with us

i've been stuck in this place

where the answers

are elusive

Tender Tulip

i've been stuck in this place

where the questions

are endless

It ends with us

i've been stuck in this place

where the unknown

is daunting

Tender Tulip

i've been stuck in this place

where the comfort

is suffocating

It ends with us

i've been stuck in this place

where the change

is terrifying

Tender Tulip

i've been stuck in this place

where the growth

is painful

It ends with us

i've been stuck in this place

where the unknown

is daunting

Tender Tulip

i've been stuck in this place

where the fear

is overwhelming

It ends with us

i've been stuck in this place

where the hope

is a faint glimmer

Tender Tulip

i've been stuck in this place

where the future

is uncertain

It ends with us

i've been stuck in this place

where the past

is haunting

i've been stuck in this place

where the present

is fleeting

Tender Tulip

i've been stuck in this place

where the hesitation

is suffocating

It ends with us

i've been stuck in this place

where the doubt

is consuming

Tender Tulip

i've been stuck in this place

where the trust

is lacking

It ends with us

i've been stuck in this place

where the love

is conditional

i've been stuck in this place

where the hate

is consuming

Tender Tulip

i've been stuck in this place

where the change

is terrifying

It ends with us

i've been stuck in this place

where the comfort

is suffocating

Tender Tulip

i've been stuck in this place

where the unknown

is daunting

It ends with us

i've been stuck in this place

where the fear

is overwhelming

Tender Tulip

i've been stuck in this place

where the hope

is a faint glimmer

i've been stuck in this place

where the future

is uncertain

It ends with us

i've been stuck in this place

where the present

is fleeting

Tender Tulip

i've been stuck in this place

where the hesitation

is suffocating

in the crossroads of uncertainty,

i stand, unsure of which path to take.

the past whispers in one ear,

while the future whispers in the other.

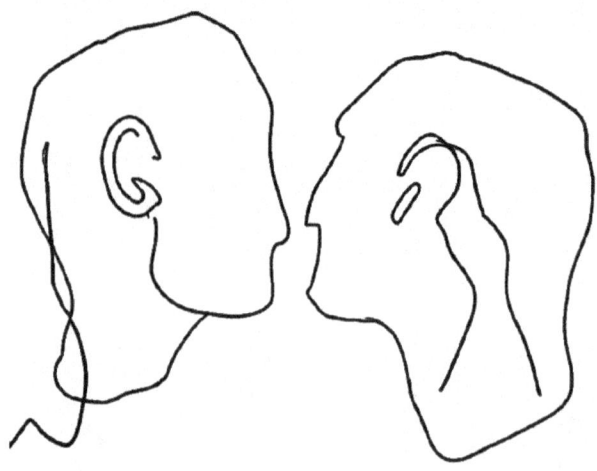

It ends with us

my mind races with a million thoughts,

fear and hope vying for attention.

i am torn between what i know,

and what could be.

Tender Tulip

i am stuck in this moment,

paralyzed by hesitation.

i long for answers,

but they elude me.

i question every decision,

doubting my ability to choose.

the unknown looms ahead,

a daunting abyss.

It ends with us

am comfortable in the familiar,

but change is necessary for growth.

but the thought of leaving my comfort zone,

terrifies me.

Tender Tulip

i am hesitant to take risks,

afraid of failure and rejection.

the future is uncertain,

and the past haunts me.

It ends with us

i am stuck in this moment,

unable to move forward.

i am stuck in a cycle of self-doubt,

hesitant to trust my own instincts.

Tender Tulip

i am hesitant to love again,

afraid of the pain that may come.

i am hesitant to let go of the old,

afraid of what the new may bring.

It ends with us

i am hesitant to let go of control,

afraid of losing myself.

i am hesitant to trust others,

afraid of being hurt again.

Tender Tulip

i am hesitant to speak my truth,

afraid of being judged.

i am hesitant to follow my heart,

afraid of the unknown.

It ends with us

but i know that hesitation

is holding me back.

i know that i must take a leap of faith,

and trust in myself.

              '

i must let go of the past,

and embrace the future.

i must let go of fear,

and embrace hope.

Tender Tulip

i must let go of control,

and trust in the journey.

i must let go of the old,

and embrace the new.

It ends with us

i must let go of hesitation,

and trust in my own strength.

i must let go of doubt,

and trust in my own ability.

Tender Tulip

i must let go of hesitation

and live my life with grace

i must trust in the journey

and let it lead the way.

It ends with us

i must let go of hesitation,

and trust in the beauty of the unknown.

for it is only then,

that i can truly live.

loneliness

It ends with us

i am the girl

who sits alone

with a heart full of sorrow

Tender Tulip

i am the girl

who feels the weight

of being misunderstood

It ends with us

i am the girl

who is surrounded

by people yet alone

Tender Tulip

i am the girl

who craves

human connection

but is too scared

to reach out

It ends with us

i am the girl

who is scared

of rejection

so i push people away

Tender Tulip

i am the girl

who is scared

of vulnerability

so i put up walls

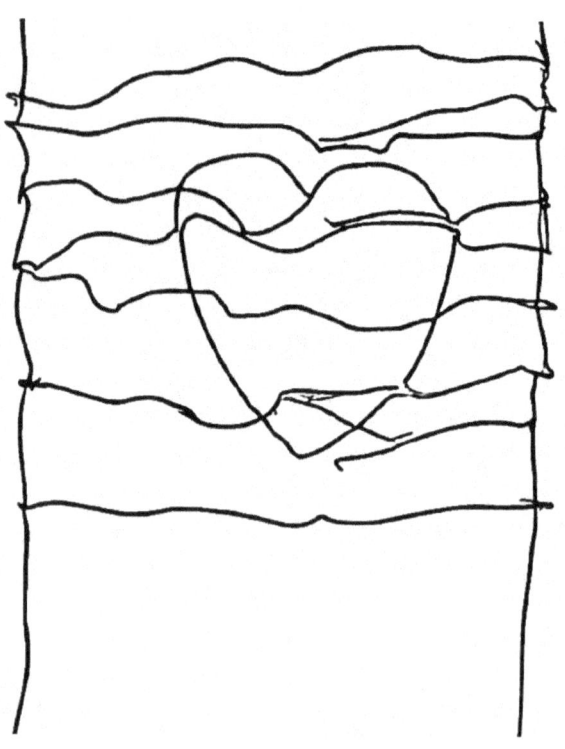

It ends with us

i am the girl

who is scared

of love

so i stay in the shadows

Tender Tulip

i am the girl

who is scared

of being hurt

so i keep my distance

It ends with us

i am the girl

who is scared

of being alone

so i hold on tight

Tender Tulip

i am the girl

who is scared

of being lonely

so i stay in the darkness

It ends with us

i am the girl

who is scared

of being known

so i hide my true self

Tender Tulip

i am the girl

who is scared

of being seen

so i hide in the shadows

It ends with us

i am the girl

who is scared

of being heard

so i stay silent

Tender Tulip

i am the girl

who is scared

of being felt

so i numb my emotions

It ends with us

i am the girl

who is scared

of being loved

so i push love away

Tender Tulip

i am the girl

who is scared

of being hurt

so i stay in the shadows

It ends with us

i am the girl

who is scared

of being lonely

so i stay in the darkness

Tender Tulip

i am the girl

who is scared

of being known

so i hide my true self

It ends with us

i am the girl

who sits with a heavy heart

surrounded by noise

but feeling so alone

Tender Tulip

i am the girl

who craves connection

but is scared to reach out

It ends with us

i am the girl

who pushes love away

afraid of being hurt

Tender Tulip

i am the girl

who numbs her emotions

afraid of being felt

It ends with us

i am the girl

who hides in the shadows

afraid of being seen

Tender Tulip

i am the girl

who stays silent

afraid of being heard

It ends with us

i am the girl

who holds on tight

afraid of being alone

Tender Tulip

i am the girl

who is scared

of the unknown

It ends with us

i am the girl

who is scared

of being rejected

i am the girl

who is scared

of being vulnerable

Tender Tulip

i am the girl

who is scared

of being hurt

It ends with us

i am the girl

who is scared

of being alone

i am the girl

who is scared

of being lonely

Tender Tulip

i am the girl

who is scared

of being known

i am the girl

who is scared

of being seen

i am the girl

who is scared

of being heard

It ends with us

i am the girl

who is scared

of being felt

Tender Tulip

i am the girl

who is scared

of being loved

but i know

that fear is holding me back

i know

that i must take a leap of faith

i must let go

of the past

It ends with us

i must let go
of fear

i must let go
of control

i must let go
of the old

i must let go
of hesitation

i must trust
in myself

i must trust
in the journey

Tender Tulip

i must trust

in the beauty

of the unknown

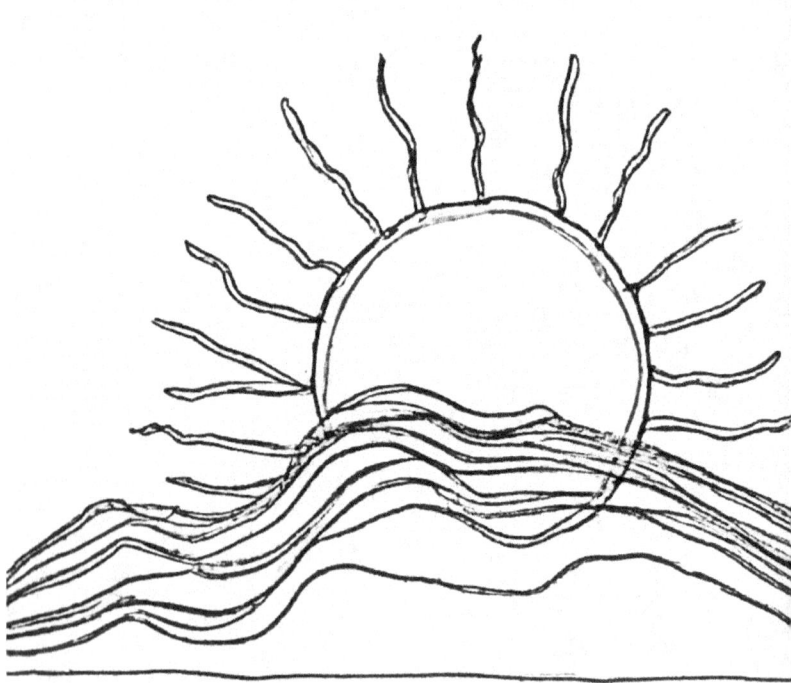

It ends with us

i must trust

in love

i must trust

in connection

i must trust

in vulnerability

Tender Tulip

i must trust

in being seen

i must trust

in being heard

i must trust

in being felt

i must trust

in being loved

i must trust

in being hurt

It ends with us

i must trust
in being alone

i must trust
in being lonely

i must trust
in being known

i must trust
in the beauty
of growth

i must trust
in the power
of my own voice

Tender Tulip

i must trust

in the journey

of self-discovery

i must trust

in the power

of healing

i must trust

in the power

of love

It ends with us

i must trust

in the power

of connection

Tender Tulip

i must trust

in the beauty

of vulnerability

i must trust

in the beauty

of being human.

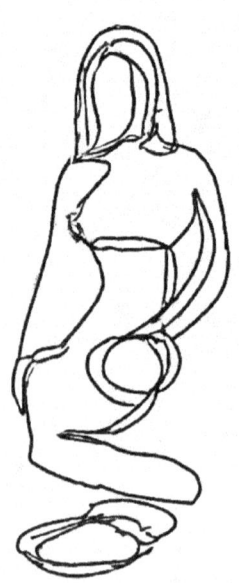

healing

Tender Tulip

i am the girl

who has been hurt

but is learning to heal

It ends with us

i am the girl

who has been broken

but is learning to mend

Tender Tulip

i am the girl

who has been shattered

but is learning to rebuild

It ends with us

i am the girl

who has been knocked down

but is learning to stand up

Tender Tulip

i am the girl

who has been scarred

but is learning to embrace the marks

It ends with us

i am the girl

who has been hurt

but is learning to forgive

i am the girl

who has been hurt

but is learning to let go

Tender Tulip

i am the girl

who has been hurt

but is learning to move on

It ends with us

i am the girl

who has been hurt

but is learning to love again

i am the girl

who has been hurt

but is learning to trust again

i am the girl

who has been hurt

but is learning to open up again

Tender Tulip

i am the girl

who has been hurt

but is learning to heal

i am the girl

who has been hurt

but is learning to forgive

i am the girl

who has been hurt

but is learning to let go

It ends with us

i am the girl

who has been hurt

but is learning to move on

i am the girl

who has been hurt

but is learning to love again

i am the girl

who has been hurt

but is learning to trust again

Tender Tulip

i am the girl

who has been hurt

but is learning to find inner peace

i am the girl

who has been hurt

but is learning to find self-love

i am the girl

who has been hurt

but is learning to find self-worth

It ends with us

i am the girl

who has been hurt

but is learning to find strength

i am the girl

who has been hurt

but is learning to find hope

i am the girl

who has been hurt

but is learning to find joy

Tender Tulip

i am the girl

who has been hurt

but is learning to find the light

i am the girl

who has been hurt

but is learning to find my voice

i am the girl

who has been hurt

but is learning to find my power

It ends with us

i am the girl

who has been hurt

but is learning to find my worth

i am the girl

who has been hurt

but is learning to find my place

i am the girl

who has been hurt

but is learning to find my purpose

Tender Tulip

i am the girl

who has been hurt

but is learning to find my way

i am the girl

who has been hurt

but is learning to find my happiness

It ends with us

i am the girl

who has been hurt

but is learning to find my freedom

i am the girl

who has been hurt

but is learning to find my healing.

it ends with us

It ends with us

the journey was long

and the road was rough

but we made it through

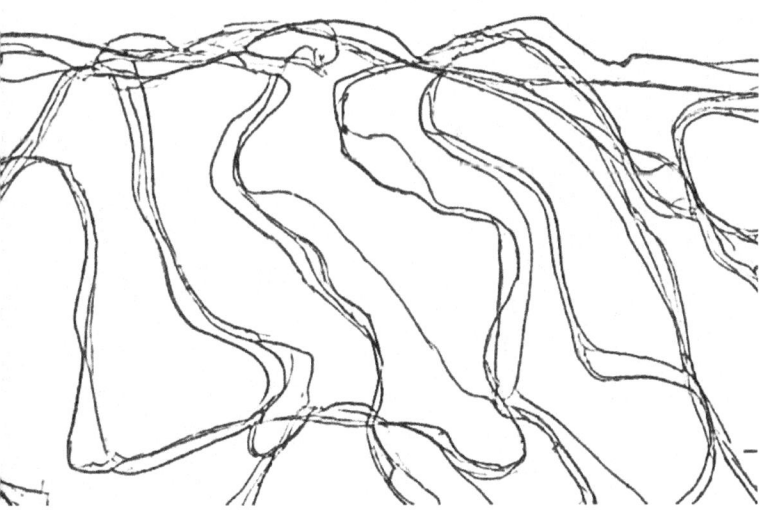

Tender Tulip

we faced our fears

and we faced our pain

we faced our past

and we faced our present

we learned to let go

of what was holding us back

It ends with us

we learned to forgive
ourselves and others

we learned to love
ourselves and others

Tender Tulip

we learned to trust

in ourselves and in the journey

we learned to find

our inner peace

It ends with us

we learned to find
our self-love

we learned to find
our self-worth

we learned to find
our strength

Tender Tulip

we learned to find

our hope

we learned to find

our joy

we learned to find

our light

It ends with us

we learned to find

our voice

we learned to find

our power

we learned to find

our place

Tender Tulip

we learned to find

our purpose

we learned to find

our way

we learned to find

our happiness

It ends with us

we learned to find

our freedom

we learned to find

our healing

we learned to find

our way home

Tender Tulip

we hope this poetry book has been a reminder
that everyone goes through struggles and
difficulties in life and that healing is possible, to
trust in oneself and the journey, to embrace the
past, present and future, to let go, forgive and
love oneself and others, and to find inner
peace, self-love, self-worth, strength, hope, joy,
light, voice, power, place, purpose, way,
happiness and freedom. we hope that this
poetry book has been a source of comfort and
inspiration for you.

about the Book

'It Ends with Us' is a moving poetry anthology concerned with themes of **recovery**, development, and introspection. The author guides the reader through the process of healing, from facing one's sorrow and fears to letting go, forgiving, and ultimately experiencing a sense of inner peace. The book is written in Rupi Kaur's signature style, which is marked by direct, accessible language, vivid imagery, and brief, unrhymed stanzas that have a strong visual effect while being accessible to readers. Poems and topics are emphasized through the recurrent usage of particular phrases and words throughout the collection. Reflection and introspection are emphasized, along with healing and the quest for self-knowledge. The book is a helpful reminder that recovery is not a destination but rather a lifelong path of self-improvement. Furthermore, it inspires readers to believe in themselves, accept their past, present, and future, let go, forgive, and love themselves and others, and ultimately discover their own unique brand of inner peace, love, worth, strength, hope, joy, light, voice, power, location, purpose, pathway, happiness, and freedom.

about The Authors

Tender Tulip is an alias used by a group of anonymous Amsterdam poets. People from all walks of life gather here to celebrate their love of poetry and encourage one another in their respective artistic pursuits. The name "Tender Tulip" was chosen to convey the community's desire to provide a warm and welcoming environment for poets of all experience levels and backgrounds. Poets in Amsterdam have a strong sense of community, and they often host poetry readings, workshops, and open mic evenings so that local poets can get their work out there. They also put out a poetry journal that welcomes writers of all stripes and serves as a forum for emerging poets. Poets of all experience levels and walks of life can count on the community to provide a welcoming and encouraging space, and members are dedicated to spreading the word about poetry's transformative potential as a means of communication.

www.ingramcontent.com/pod-product-compliance
Lightning Source LLC
Chambersburg PA
CBHW071359120626
46546CB00002B/748